Key Stage 1

Maths Revision Guide

Hilary Koll and Steve Mills

Schofield&Sims

Welcome to this book

This book will help you revise the maths you have learnt in Years 1 and 2.

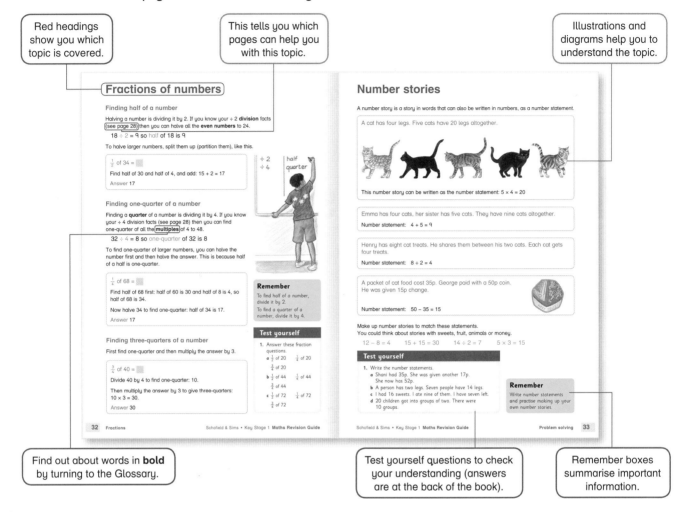

Red headings show you which topic is covered.

This tells you which pages can help you with this topic.

Illustrations and diagrams help you to understand the topic.

Find out about words in **bold** by turning to the Glossary.

Test yourself questions to check your understanding (answers are at the back of the book).

Remember boxes summarise important information.

How to revise

- Turn to the topic and read about it.
- Read the Remember box and then cover it up. Can you remember what it says?
- Read the Test yourself questions and write your answers on a piece of paper.
- Check your answers against the right answers at the back of the book.
- If you got any answers wrong, read the topic again, then have another go at the questions.
- If you got the answers right – well done! Move on to the next topic.
- Once you have worked through this revision guide, move on to the **Key Stage 1 Maths Practice Papers**.

Tips for tests

- Always read the question carefully before you answer it.
- Have a go at as many questions as you can. If there is a question you really can't answer, just move on to the next one. You can always come back to it if you have time.
- Try to get an idea of what the answer should be before you work it out.
- If you have time at the end, check through your work.

Contents

Numbers and digits

Each number is made from one or more **digits**.

This number has one digit. This number has two digits. This number has three digits.

6 **27** **354**

Numbers in digits and in words

These numbers are written in digits and words. Watch out for difficult spellings like 'eight' and 'forty'.

1	2	3	4	5	6	7	8	9	10
one	two	three	four	five	six	seven	eight	nine	ten

11	12	13	14	15	16	17	18	19	20
eleven	twelve	thirteen	fourteen	fifteen	sixteen	seventeen	eighteen	nineteen	twenty

21	22	23	24	25	26	27	28	29	30
twenty-one	twenty-two	twenty-three	twenty-four	twenty-five	twenty-six	twenty-seven	twenty-eight	twenty-nine	thirty

Other numbers include:

40	50	60	70	80	90	100	200	300
forty	fifty	sixty	seventy	eighty	ninety	one hundred	two hundred	three hundred

1000	2000	3000	4000	5000	6000	7000	8000	9000
one thousand	two thousand	three thousand	four thousand	five thousand	six thousand	seven thousand	eight thousand	nine thousand

Test yourself

1. Write these numbers in words.
   a 12 **b** 24 **c** 36 **d** 84 **e** 18 **f** 48 **g** 100

2. Write these numbers in digits.
   a thirteen **c** fifty-two **e** three thousand
   b two hundred **d** ninety-five **f** sixty

Remember

All numbers are made from one or more digits.

Odd and even numbers

Look at these flip-flops.

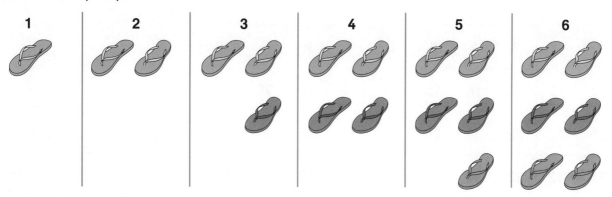

The numbers 1, 3 and 5 have an odd number of flip-flops.
1, 3 and 5 are called **odd numbers**.

The numbers 2, 4 and 6 have pairs of flip-flops and no odd ones.
2, 4 and 6 are called **even numbers**.

Every whole number is either even or odd.

Even numbers

2, 4, 6, 8, 10, 12, 14, 16, 18 and 20 are all even numbers.

Any number that is divided by 2 without a **remainder** is an even number.
All even numbers end in 0, 2, 4, 6 or 8.

> Is the number 16 even?
>
> $16 \div 2 = 8$ ◀—— There is no remainder, so 16 is an even number.

Odd numbers

1, 3, 5, 7, 9, 11, 13, 15, 17 and 19 are all odd numbers.

Any number that is divided by 2 and has a remainder of 1 is an odd number.
All odd numbers end in 1, 3, 5, 7 or 9.

> Is the number 17 odd?
>
> $17 \div 2 = 8$ remainder 1 ◀—— There is a remainder, so 17 is an odd number.

Test yourself

1. Say whether each number is odd or even.
   a 6 **b** 3 **c** 9 **d** 12 **e** 18 **f** 25 **g** 54 **h** 67

2. Which of these numbers are odd?
   123, 566, 462, 388, 482, 698, 659, 597, 365, 471, 600

Remember

All even numbers end in 0, 2, 4, 6 or 8.

All odd numbers end in 1, 3, 5, 7 or 9.

Counting in ones

You can use a hundred square to help you count in ones.

1	2	3	4	5	6	7	8	9	10
11	12	13	14	15	16	17	18	19	20
21	22	23	24	25	26	27	28	29	30
31	32	33	34	35	36	37	38	39	40
41	42	43	44	45	46	47	48	49	50
51	52	53	54	55	56	57	58	59	60
61	62	63	64	65	66	67	68	69	70
71	72	73	74	75	76	77	78	79	80
81	82	83	84	85	86	87	88	89	90
91	92	93	94	95	96	97	98	99	100

Point to number 1 in this hundred square. Count slowly in ones, pointing to each number as you say it aloud. How far can you count forwards?

1, 2, 3, 4, 5, 6, 7, 8, 9...

Start from the number 55 and count backwards in ones. How far can you count backwards?

55, 54, 53, 52, 51, 50, 49...

Find the next three numbers in this pattern by counting on or back

17, 18, 19, 20, ___, ___, ___

Answer 21, 22, 23

Test yourself

1. Find the next three numbers in these patterns.
   a 36, 37, 38, 39, ___, ___, ___
   b 73, 72, 71, 70, ___, ___, ___
   c 85, 86, 87, 88, ___, ___, ___
   d 100, 99, 98, 97, ___, ___, ___

Remember

Practise counting on and back in ones from any number up to 100.

Counting in twos

Counting every other number is called counting in twos.

Count forwards in twos from the number 2.

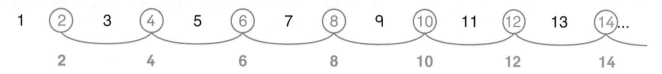

1 ② 3 ④ 5 ⑥ 7 ⑧ 9 ⑩ 11 ⑫ 13 ⑭...

   2   4   6   8   10   12   14

You can begin on any number.

1 2 3 4 5 6 ⑦ 8 ⑨ 10 ⑪ 12 ⑬ 14...

                    7   9   11   13

Now try counting backwards in twos, like this.

32, 30, 28, 26, 24, 22, 20, 18, 16...

63, 61, 59, 57, 55, 53, 51, 49, 47...

Odd and even numbers

Counting in twos from an odd number	Counting in twos from an even number
Notice that when you count in twos, starting from an **odd number**, all the numbers will be odd.	When you count in twos, starting from an **even number**, all the numbers will be even.
5, 7, 9, 11, 13, 15, 17, 19...	4, 6, 8, 10, 12, 14, 16, 18...
55, 53, 51, 49, 47, 45, 43...	78, 76, 74, 72, 70, 68, 66...

See page 5 for more about odd and even numbers.

Test yourself

1. Count on in twos from 46 to 76.

2. Count back in twos from 53 to 37.

3. Find the next three numbers.
   a 36, 38, 40, 42, ___, ___, ___
   b 75, 73, 71, 69, ___, ___, ___
   c 81, 83, 85, 87, ___, ___, ___
   d 100, 98, 96, 94, ___, ___, ___

Remember

Practise counting on and back in twos from any number up to 100.

Counting in tens

In this hundred square, numbers are in rows of ten. Look down a column when counting on in tens.

When you count on in tens, the tens **digit** grows by one each time.

1	2	3	4	5	6	7	8	9	10
11	12	13	14	15	16	17	18	19	20
21	22	23	24	25	26	27	28	29	30
31	32	33	34	35	36	37	38	39	40
41	42	43	44	45	46	47	48	49	50
51	52	53	54	55	56	57	58	59	60
61	62	63	64	65	66	67	68	69	70
71	72	73	74	75	76	77	78	79	80
81	82	83	84	85	86	87	88	89	90
91	92	93	94	95	96	97	98	99	100

```
tens  ones
  5    2
+ 1    0
  6    2
```

The tens digit gets one larger and the ones digit stays the same.

Counting on from 6

Use the hundred square to count on in tens from 6. You will see that the ones digit is always 6.

   6, 16, 26, 36, 46, 56...

Counting on from 2

Now find the column starting with the number 2 and count on in tens from 2.

   2, 12, 22, 32, 42, 52...

```
tens  ones
  5    2
− 1    0
  4    2
```

When you count back in tens, the tens digit gets smaller by one each time.

The tens digit gets one smaller and the ones digit stays the same.

10

Test yourself

1. Count on in tens from 26 to 96.

2. Count back in tens from 87 to 7.

3. Find the next three numbers in these patterns.
   a 38, 48, 58, 68, ___, ___, ___
   b 99, 89, 79, 69, ___, ___, ___

Remember

When you count in tens, the ones digit always stays the same.

Counting in fives

When counting in fives, notice the pattern in the ones digits.

5, 10, 15, 20, 25, 30, 35, 40…

Each of these numbers is a **multiple** of 5. They are numbers in the 5 times table or beyond. All multiples of 5 end in 0 or 5. (For more about multiples, see page 26.)

When counting from other numbers, you can also see patterns in the ones digits.

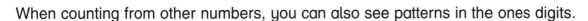

Counting on in fives from 2

2, 7, 12, 17, 22, 27, 32, 37…

The ones digits are 2 or 7.

Counting back in fives from 94

94, 89, 84, 79, 74, 69, 64, 59…

The ones digits are 4 or 9.

Now it's your turn. Count on in fives from 1 on the hundred square.

1, 6, 11, 16, 21, 26…
(The ones digits are 1 or 6.)

1	2	3	4	5	6	7	8	9	10
11	12	13	14	15	16	17	18	19	20
21	22	23	24	25	26	27	28	29	30
31	32	33	34	35	36	37	38	39	40
41	42	43	44	45	46	47	48	49	50
51	52	53	54	55	56	57	58	59	60
61	62	63	64	65	66	67	68	69	70
71	72	73	74	75	76	77	78	79	80
81	82	83	84	85	86	87	88	89	90
91	92	93	94	95	96	97	98	99	100

Test yourself

1. Find the next three numbers in these patterns.
   a 38, 43, 48, 53, ___, ___, ___
   b 95, 90, 85, 80, ___, ___, ___
   c 47, 52, 57, 62, ___, ___, ___

Remember

When you count on or back in fives, every other ones digit is the same.

Counting in threes

When counting in threes, use a 'whisper, whisper, SHOUT' approach at first:

1, 2, 3, 4, 5, 6, 7, 8, 9, 10, 11, 12, 13, 14, 15, 16, 17, 18…

After a while, just say:

3, 6, 9, 12, 15, 18…

When you add the **digits** of a **multiple** of 3, you get another multiple of 3.
(For more about multiples, see page 26.)

24 is a multiple of 3 ⟵ 2 + 4 = 6 (6 is a multiple of 3)

45 is a multiple of 3 ⟵ 4 + 5 = 9 (9 is a multiple of 3)

Look at the multiples of 3 in this hundred square. Check the sum of the digits and look for patterns in the answers.

Add the digits of numbers that are not multiples of 3. You will notice that they do not give a multiple of 3.

1	2	3	4	5	6	7	8	9	10
11	12	13	14	15	16	17	18	19	20
21	22	23	24	25	26	27	28	29	30
31	32	33	34	35	36	37	38	39	40
41	42	43	44	45	46	47	48	49	50
51	52	53	54	55	56	57	58	59	60
61	62	63	64	65	66	67	68	69	70
71	72	73	74	75	76	77	78	79	80
81	82	83	84	85	86	87	88	89	90
91	92	93	94	95	96	97	98	99	100

Test yourself

1. Count on in threes from 15 to 39.

2. Count back in threes from 87 to 60.

3. Which number in this set is a multiple of 3? 62, 48, 50

Remember

When the digits of a multiple of 3 (such as 15) are added together (in this case 1 + 5) they equal another multiple of 3 (in this case 6).

Comparing numbers

To show which number is larger or smaller, use the 'less than' and 'greater than' signs.

less than

greater than

Which is larger, 3 or 7? Use the < or > sign

7 is larger than 3, so you need to use the 'greater than' sign.

Answer **7 > 3**

Which is smaller, 3 or 7? Use the < or > sign

3 is smaller than 7, so you need to use the 'less than' sign.

Answer **3 < 7**

To show that two numbers are the same, use the = sign.

equals

Use <, > or = to complete the following: 3 __ 3

3 is the same as 3, so you need to use the equals sign.

Answer **3 = 3**

You can also think of these comparisons as pictures.

    3 7   3 3

Some people think of the < and > signs as a crocodile's mouth, about to eat the larger number.

Test yourself

1. Use < or > to complete the following.
  a 4 __ 9
  b 6 __ 2
  c 8 __ 14
  d 22 __ 16

2. Use <, > or = to complete the following.
  a 7 __ 6
  b 8 __ 8
  c 12 __ 19
  d 26 __ 16

Remember

The wider part of the < or > sign is always next to the larger number.

Ordering

Ordering numbers to 100

When ordering numbers to 100, make sure you know what each **digit** stands for, like tens and ones.

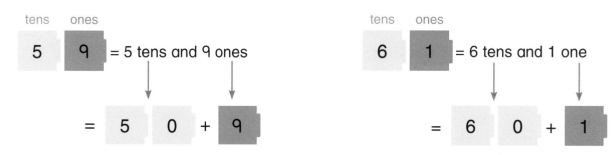

tens	ones
5	9	= 5 tens and 9 ones

= 5 0 + 9

tens	ones
6	1	= 6 tens and 1 one

= 6 0 + 1

Which is larger, 59 or 61? Use the < or > sign.

61 has 6 tens and 59 has only 5 tens, so 61 is larger than 59. The < sign shows that 59 is smaller than 61.

Answer 59 < 61

Put these numbers in order, starting with the smallest:
58, 71, 19, 42, 80

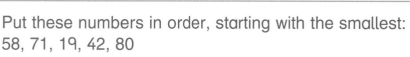

19   42   58   71   80

| 10 + 9 | 40 + 2 | 50 + 8 | 70 + 1 | 80 + 0 |

Answer 19, 42, 58, 71, 80

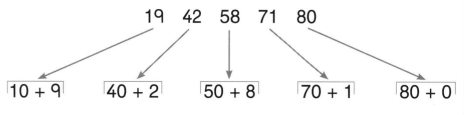
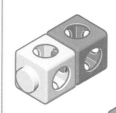

Test yourself

1. Order these numbers, starting with the smallest.
   a 52, 64, 73, 13, 39   **b** 47, 69, 42, 79, 21

2. How many tens has each of these numbers?
   a 59   **b** 32

3. Split these numbers into parts.
   a 46 = 40 + 6   **b** 84 =   **c** 93 =

4. Write < or > to show which is larger.
   a 45 ___ 54   **b** 81 ___ 76

Remember

When ordering numbers, make sure you know what each digit in the number stands for.

Ordering numbers to 1000

When ordering numbers to 1000, make sure you know what each digit stands for, like hundreds, tens and ones.

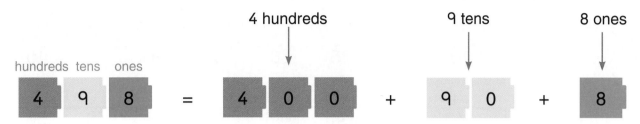

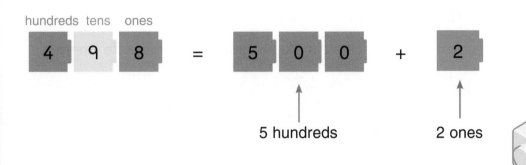

Which number is larger, 498 or 502?

502 has 5 hundreds and 498 only has 4 hundreds, so 502 is larger than 498.

Answer **502**

Put these numbers in order, starting with the smallest: 490, 362, 500, 946, 601

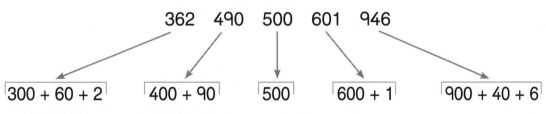

Answer **362, 490, 500, 601, 946**

Test yourself

1. Order these, starting with the smallest.
   a 72, 644, 743, 193, 379 **b** 487, 629, 411, 709, 251

2. How many hundreds has each of these numbers?
   a 589 **b** 732 **c** 295

3. Split these numbers into parts.
   a 146 = *100 + 40 + 6*   **c** 721 =
   b 439 =   **d** 297 =

Remember

When ordering numbers, make sure you know what each digit in the number stands for – hundreds, tens or ones.

Number lines

Numbers can be arranged on number lines, like these.

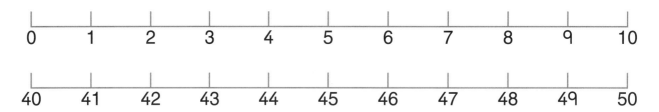

Estimating numbers on number lines

Sometimes not all the numbers are marked, like this. You might need to **estimate** where a number is on the line.

Estimate the number the arrow is pointing to

To make a good estimate, split the line into equal parts. Then mark on other numbers.

about 75

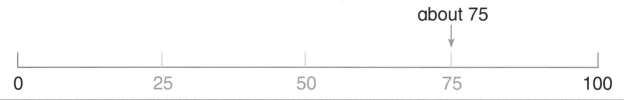

Always look carefully at the numbers. They might not start at zero.
In this example, the arrow is pointing to about 35.

Test yourself

1. Estimate the numbers that these arrows are pointing to.

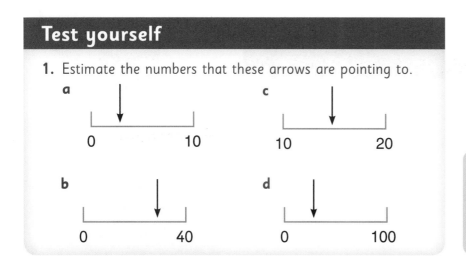

Remember

Split the line into equal parts to help you make a good estimate.

Number patterns

When you count on in equal steps, you make a pattern or **sequence**. In the examples below there is a pattern, but some numbers are missing.

Find the missing number in this pattern

| 2 | 4 | 6 | 8 | | 12 | 14 |

Is the pattern going up or down?

Is the pattern going in 1s, 2s, 5s or 10s or other-sized steps?

2   4   6   8   ___   12   14

This pattern is going up in 2s. The missing number must be 2 more than 8.

Answer 10

Find the missing number in this pattern

| 83 | 73 | 63 | | 43 | 33 |

This pattern is going down in 10s. The missing number must be 10 less than 63 and 10 more than 43.

Answer 53

Find the missing two numbers in this pattern

| 7 | 12 | 17 | | 27 | | 37 |

This pattern is going up in 5s. The missing numbers must be:

5 more than 17, which is 22

5 more than 27, which is 32

Answers 22, 32

Test yourself

1. Find the missing numbers.
  a 3, 5, 7, ___, 11, 13
  b 2, 12, 22, ___, ___, 52
  c 67, 65, ___, 61, ___, 57
  d 8, 13, ___, 23, 28, ___

Remember

Ask: is the pattern going up or down? Is it going in 1s, 2s, 5s or 10s, or other-sized steps?

Mental addition

These words usually mean you need to do an **addition**.

more   add   total   plus   altogether   sum   and

This sign + means add. For example, 12 + 7 = 19

Splitting numbers up for addition

Numbers can be split up, like 26 into 20 and 6. This is called partioning.

It can make addition easier.

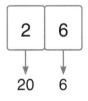

| 2 | 6 |

20 6

Add 26 and 13

First, split up the numbers.

| 2 | 6 | + | 1 | 3 |

20 + 6   10 + 3

Then add the tens.	20 + 10 = 30
Next add the ones.	6 + 3 = 9
Then add the total tens to the total ones.	30 + 9 = 39

Answer 39

Test yourself

1. Split these numbers into tens and ones.
   a 29   b 46   c 78

2. Add these numbers:
   a 27 + 12   b 16 + 25   c 26 + 37

Remember

Split numbers into tens and ones to make addition easier.

Adding 10

When adding 10, just add 1 to the tens column.

$$39 + 10 = 49$$
$$75 + 10 = 85$$

Adding 100

When adding 100, just add 1 to the hundreds column.

$$247 + 100 = 347$$
$$582 + 100 = 682$$

Adding three numbers

Here are two different ways of adding three numbers.

1. Find pairs that add to 10 and add these first

Add 3 + 5 + 7

Look at   3   +   5   +   7

You know that 3 + 7 = 10, so just do   3   +   7   +   5   = 15

Answer 15

2. Start with the largest number first

Add 4 + 8 + 3

Look at   4   +   8   +   3

8 is the biggest. 4 is the next biggest. So just do   8   +   4   +   3   = 15

Answer 15

Test yourself

1. Add 10 to these numbers.
   a 43   b 58

2. Add 100 to these numbers.
   a 145   b 387

3. Add these numbers.
   a 5 + 6 + 4   b 6 + 7 + 9

Remember

When adding three numbers, you can change the order to make it easier.

Always look for pairs that add to 10.

Written addition

It is helpful to write numbers in columns for **addition**.

Adding two-digit numbers

When writing the numbers, make sure that the ones **digits** line up with ones digits, tens with tens digits and so on.

Add 43 and 25

Start with the ones: 3 + 5 = 8
Then add the tens: 4 + 2 = 6

```
        tens ones

           4    3

    +      2    5
         ─────────
           6    8
         ─────────
```

Answer **68**

Sometimes the number of ones is more than 9, so you will need to carry a ten across to the tens column.

Add 47 and 27

Start with the ones: 7 + 7 is 14
Write the 4 in the ones column and carry the ten across to be 1 ten in the tens column.
Add the tens: 4 + 2, plus the 1 carried is 7

```
        tens ones

           4    7

    +      2    7
         ─────────
           7    4
         ─────────
             1
```

Answer **74**

Test yourself

1. Use written addition to find the answers to these questions.
   a 53 + 42 =
   b 26 + 63 =
   c 37 + 48 =

2. What is the missing digit in this sum?

```
           4    5

    +      3    ▩
         ─────────
           8    3
         ─────────
```

When the total is greater than 100, you need to use the hundreds column.

> ## Add 63 and 65
>
> Start with the ones: 3 + 5 = 8
> Then add the tens: 6 tens + 6 tens is 12 tens.
> Carry the 1 into the hundreds column and write the 2 in the tens column.
>
> | | hundreds | tens | ones |
> |---|---|---|---|
> | | | 6 | 3 |
> | + | | 6 | 5 |
> | | 1 | 2 | 8 |
> | | | 1 | |
>
> Answer **128**

Adding three-digit numbers

You add three-digit numbers in the same way.

> ## Add 578 and 34
>
> Write in the digits correctly first.
> Then start by adding the ones: 8 + 4 = 12
> Carry the 1 into the tens column and add it to the 7 tens and 3 tens to get 11.
> Carry the 1 into the hundreds column.
> 5 + 1 = 6 to complete the answer.
>
> | | hundreds | tens | ones |
> |---|---|---|---|
> | | 5 | 7 | 8 |
> | + | | 3 | 4 |
> | | 6 | 1 | 2 |
> | | | 1 | 1 |
>
> Answer **612**

Remember

In written addition, start by adding the ones, then the tens, then the hundreds – and so on.

Test yourself

1. Use written addition to find the answers.
   a 63 + 46 =
   b 57 + 94 =
   c 446 + 71 =
   d 327 + 144 =

2. What are the missing digits in this sum?

	6	4	6
+		9	▮
	▮	4	3

Mental subtraction

These words usually mean you need to do a **subtraction**.

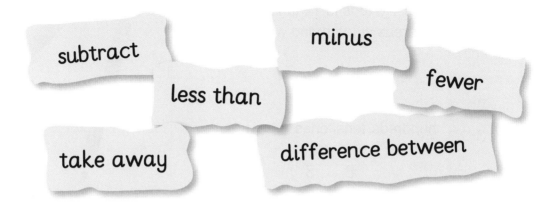

This sign − means subtract. For example, 12 − 7 = 5

Splitting numbers up for subtraction

Numbers can be split up, like 18 into 10 and 8. This is called partitioning. It can make subtraction easier.

1	8

↓   ↓
10   8

---

35 subtract 18

3	5	−	1	8

↓   ↓
10   8

Subtract the tens.   35 − 10 = 25

Then subtract the ones.   25 − 8 = 17

Answer 17

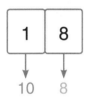

Test yourself

1. Which are addition and which are subtraction words?
   a more   b minus   c fewer   d altogether

2. Subtract these.
   a 54 − 13   b 65 − 24   c 73 − 27

Remember

Split numbers to make subtraction easier.

Subtracting 10

When subtracting 10, just take 1 from the tens column.

$$48 - 10 = 38$$
$$67 - 10 = 57$$

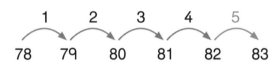

Subtracting 100

When subtracting 100, just take 1 from the hundreds column.

$$537 - 100 = 437$$
$$946 - 100 = 846$$

Finding the difference

Here are two ways to find the difference between numbers.

1. Counting on

> Find the difference between 78 and 83
>
> Count on from 78 to 83
>
> 1   2   3   4   5
>
> 78   79   80   81   82   83
>
> The difference between 78 and 83 is 5.
>
> Answer **5**

2. Using a blank number line

> Find the difference between 78 and 83
>
> Use a blank number line with 80 as a 'stepping stone'.
>
> 2   3
>
> 78   80   83
>
> $$2 + 3 = 5$$
>
> The difference between 78 and 83 is 5.
>
> Answer **5**

Test yourself

1. Subtract 10 from these numbers.
   a 67
   b 76
   c 89

2. Subtract 100 from these numbers.
   a 375
   b 603
   c 999

3. Find the difference between these numbers.
   a 58 and 63
   b 47 and 54
   c 65 and 72

Remember

You can find the difference between numbers by counting on.

Written subtraction

It is helpful to write numbers in columns for **subtraction**.

Subtracting two-digit numbers

Make sure that the ones **digits** line up in the ones column, the tens in the tens column and so on.

Subtract 25 from 89

When subtracting, start with the ones: 9 – 5 = 4
Then subtract the tens: 8 – 2 = 6

```
     tens  ones

       8    9

  –    2    5
     _____

       6    4
     _____
```

Answer **64**

In 63 – 27, the ones in the first number (3) are less than the second number (7). You need to borrow a 1 from the tens column, so that there are 13 rather than 3 ones.

Subtract 27 from 63

First subtract the ones: 13 – 7 is 6
Then subtract the tens: 5 – 2 = 3

```
     tens  ones

       6⁵   ¹3

  –    2    7
     _____

       3    6
     _____
```

Answer **36**

Remember

Write numbers in columns for written subtraction.

Test yourself

1. Use written subtraction to find the answers to these questions.
   a 53 – 42 =
   b 96 – 63 =
   c 84 – 48 =

2. What is the missing digit in this subtraction?

```
       9    5

  –    3    ▨
     _____

       5    9
     _____
```

Subtracting with three-digit numbers

You can subtract three-digit numbers in the same way.
Borrow from the column to the left, if you need to.

Subtract 573 from 949

First subtract the ones: 9 − 3 = 6
Then subtract the tens.
Here there are only 4 tens and you need to take away 7.

Borrow 1 from the hundreds column so that you have 14
tens: 14 − 7 = 7
Then subtract the hundreds: 8 − 5 = 3

	hundreds	tens	ones
	$9̷^8$	^{14}	9
−	5	7	3
	3	7	6

Answer **376**

Subtract 87 from 478

Notice how to write 478 − 87 in the correct columns.
First subtract the ones: 8 − 7 = 1
Then subtract the tens.
Here there are only 7 tens and you need to take away 8.

Borrow 1 from the hundreds column so that you have
17 tens: 17 − 8 = 9
Then subtract the hundreds: 3 − 0 = 3

	hundreds	tens	ones
	$4̷^3$	^{17}	8
−		8	7
	3	9	1

Answer **391**

Remember

In written subtraction, start by subtracting the ones, then the tens, then the hundreds — and so on.

Test yourself

1. Use written subtraction to find the answers.
   a 567 − 245 =
   b 846 − 128 =
   c 737 − 258 =
   d 614 − 573 =

2. What are the missing digits?

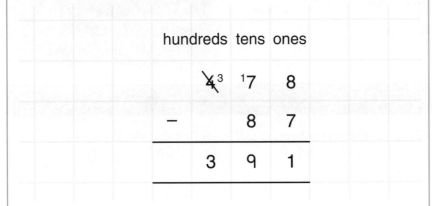

	3	9	4
−		3	▢
	3	▢	9

Addition and subtraction facts

Knowing **addition** facts that total 10, 20 and 100 will help you to work in your head more easily. Try to learn all the facts on this page.

Addition facts that total 10

0 + 10 = 10	3 + 7 = 10	5 + 5 = 10	7 + 3 = 10	9 + 1 = 10
1 + 9 = 10	4 + 6 = 10	6 + 4 = 10	8 + 2 = 10	10 + 0 = 10
2 + 8 = 10				

Addition facts that total 20

0 + 20 = 20	5 + 15 = 20	9 + 11 = 20	13 + 7 = 20	17 + 3 = 20
1 + 19 = 20	6 + 14 = 20	10 + 10 = 20	14 + 6 = 20	18 + 2 = 20
2 + 18 = 20	7 + 13 = 20	11 + 9 = 20	15 + 5 = 20	19 + 1 = 20
3 + 17 = 20	8 + 12 = 20	12 + 8 = 20	16 + 4 = 20	20 + 0 = 20
4 + 16 = 20				

Addition facts that total 100

10 + 90 = 100	40 + 60 = 100	70 + 30 = 100
20 + 80 = 100	50 + 50 = 100	80 + 20 = 100
30 + 70 = 100	60 + 40 = 100	90 + 10 = 100

Subtraction facts

If you know an addition fact, then you also know some **subtraction** facts.

11 + 9 = 20	20 − 11 = 9	20 − 9 = 11

You can use this to find missing numbers.

To find: ▨ + 7 = 23   subtract 7 from 23

To find: ▨ − 9 = 16   add 9 to 16

> **Remember**
>
> If you know an addition fact then you also know some subtraction facts.

Test yourself

1. Find these numbers.
   a ▨ + 4 = 10
   b 9 + ▨ = 10
   c ▨ + 8 = 10
   d 3 + ▨ = 10

2. Find these numbers.
   a 11 + ▨ = 20
   b ▨ + 4 = 20
   c 13 + ▨ = 20
   d ▨ + 12 = 20

3. Find these numbers.
   a 80 + ▨ = 100
   b ▨ + 40 = 100
   c 30 + ▨ = 100

Multiplication

Multiplication helps you to add more quickly.

You multiply or 'times' one number by another.

These peppers come in packs of three. There are four packs of peppers. How many peppers are there?

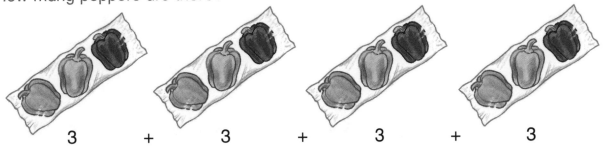

3   +   3   +   3   +   3

This can be written as four times three or four multiplied by three.

4 lots of 3   or   4 × 3

If you know the tables fact   4 × 3 = 12   then you don't need to add.

Answer **12 peppers**

Here are 8 five pence coins. How much money is there?

5   +   5   +   5   +   5   +   5   +   5   +   5   +   5

This can be written as:

8 lots of 5   or   8 × 5

If you know the tables fact   8 × 5 = 40   then you don't need to add.

Answer **40p**

Test yourself

1. Write these questions as multiplication questions.
   a 2 + 2 + 2 + 2 = 4 x 2
   b 5 + 5 + 5 + 5 =
   c 3 + 3 + 3 + 3 + 3 =
   d 4 + 4 + 4 =

Remember

Multiplication helps you to add more quickly.

Learn your tables facts (see next page) to save even more time.

Times tables facts

You will find **multiplication** much easier if you learn your times tables facts.

× 2	× 3	× 4	× 5	× 10
1 × 2 = 2	1 × 3 = 3	1 × 4 = 4	1 × 5 = 5	1 × 10 = 10
2 × 2 = 4	2 × 3 = 6	2 × 4 = 8	2 × 5 = 10	2 × 10 = 20
3 × 2 = 6	3 × 3 = 9	3 × 4 = 12	3 × 5 = 15	3 × 10 = 30
4 × 2 = 8	4 × 3 = 12	4 × 4 = 16	4 × 5 = 20	4 × 10 = 40
5 × 2 = 10	5 × 3 = 15	5 × 4 = 20	5 × 5 = 25	5 × 10 = 50
6 × 2 = 12	6 × 3 = 18	6 × 4 = 24	6 × 5 = 30	6 × 10 = 60
7 × 2 = 14	7 × 3 = 21	7 × 4 = 28	7 × 5 = 35	7 × 10 = 70
8 × 2 = 16	8 × 3 = 24	8 × 4 = 32	8 × 5 = 40	8 × 10 = 80
9 × 2 = 18	9 × 3 = 27	9 × 4 = 36	9 × 5 = 45	9 × 10 = 90
10 × 2 = 20	10 × 3 = 30	10 × 4 = 40	10 × 5 = 50	10 × 10 = 100
11 × 2 = 22	11 × 3 = 33	11 × 4 = 44	11 × 5 = 55	11 × 10 = 110
12 × 2 = 24	12 × 3 = 36	12 × 4 = 48	12 × 5 = 60	12 × 10 = 120

---

5 × 2 = 10

Look at the two facts in blue.

5 × 2 has the same answer as 2 × 5

---

10 × 3 = 30

Look at the two facts in green.

10 × 3 has the same answer as 3 × 10

Switching around the numbers

The numbers in any tables fact can be switched around and the answer will be the same.

2 × 5 = 10 ⟶ 5 × 2 = 10

3 × 4 = 12 ⟶ 4 × 3 = 12

5 × 3 = 15 ⟶ 3 × 5 = 15

4 × 10 = 40 ⟶ 10 × 4 = 40

This means that for every fact you learn, you also learn another fact!

Multiples

A tables fact answer is always called a **multiple**.

40 is a multiple of 4 because it is in the × 4 table.
It is also a multiple of 10 because it is in the × 10 table.

Remember

The numbers in any tables fact can be switched around and the answer will be the same.

Test yourself

1. Cover the page and see how many of these answers you know.

2 × 3	3 × 5
5 × 10	4 × 2
6 × 3	7 × 10
8 × 2	6 × 5
9 × 4	7 × 3
6 × 10	5 × 4
3 × 3	8 × 5

Division

Division is about sharing or sorting things into groups.

Sharing

6 ÷ 2 (6 divided by 2) can be thought of as 6 shared between 2.

Share six apples between two bowls

Answer Each bowl holds 3 so $6 ÷ 2 = 3$

Grouping

6 ÷ 2 (6 divided by 2) can also be thought of as 6 grouped into 2s.

Sort these six parrots into groups of twos

Answer There are 3 groups altogether so $6 ÷ 2 = 3$

You can use either sharing or grouping to answer division questions like the one below.

Find the answer to 8 ÷ 2

Sharing	**Grouping**
Share 8 sweets between 2 boys.	Group 8 sweets into groups of 2.
How many do they get each?	How many groups are there?
Answer 4	Answer 4

Test yourself

1. Answer these using sharing.
   a   4 ÷ 2
   b   6 ÷ 3
   c 12 ÷ 4
   d 15 ÷ 5

2. Answer these using grouping.
   a 10 ÷ 2
   b   9 ÷ 3
   c 12 ÷ 3
   d 20 ÷ 5

Remember

You can divide using sharing or grouping. For larger numbers it is often easier to use grouping.

Division facts

Division is much easier if you learn division facts. Division facts are like times tables facts, but the other way round.

Look at these times tables facts. $3 \times 4 = 12$ and $4 \times 3 = 12$

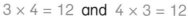

These division facts are also related. $12 \div 3 = 4$ and $12 \div 4 = 3$

÷ 2	÷ 3	÷ 4	÷ 5	÷ 10
$2 \div 2 = 1$	$3 \div 3 = 1$	$4 \div 4 = 1$	$5 \div 5 = 1$	$10 \div 10 = 1$
$4 \div 2 = 2$	$6 \div 3 = 2$	$8 \div 4 = 2$	$10 \div 5 = 2$	$20 \div 10 = 2$
$6 \div 2 = 3$	$9 \div 3 = 3$	$12 \div 4 = 3$	$15 \div 5 = 3$	$30 \div 10 = 3$
$8 \div 2 = 4$	$12 \div 3 = 4$	$16 \div 4 = 4$	$20 \div 5 = 4$	$40 \div 10 = 4$
$10 \div 2 = 5$	$15 \div 3 = 5$	$20 \div 4 = 5$	$25 \div 5 = 5$	$50 \div 10 = 5$
$12 \div 2 = 6$	$18 \div 3 = 6$	$24 \div 4 = 6$	$30 \div 5 = 6$	$60 \div 10 = 6$
$14 \div 2 = 7$	$21 \div 3 = 7$	$28 \div 4 = 7$	$35 \div 5 = 7$	$70 \div 10 = 7$
$16 \div 2 = 8$	$24 \div 3 = 8$	$32 \div 4 = 8$	$40 \div 5 = 8$	$80 \div 10 = 8$
$18 \div 2 = 9$	$27 \div 3 = 9$	$36 \div 4 = 9$	$45 \div 5 = 9$	$90 \div 10 = 9$
$20 \div 2 = 10$	$30 \div 3 = 10$	$40 \div 4 = 10$	$50 \div 5 = 10$	$100 \div 10 = 10$
$22 \div 2 = 11$	$33 \div 3 = 11$	$44 \div 4 = 11$	$55 \div 5 = 11$	$110 \div 10 = 11$
$24 \div 2 = 12$	$36 \div 3 = 12$	$48 \div 4 = 12$	$60 \div 5 = 12$	$120 \div 10 = 12$

Switching around the numbers

The numbers in division facts can be switched around, like these. Look at the examples below. This means that for every fact you learn, you also learn another fact!

$15 \div 3 = 5 \longrightarrow 15 \div 5 = 3$ $40 \div 10 = 4 \longrightarrow 40 \div 4 = 10$

Test yourself

1. Cover the division facts to see how many you know.

$6 \div 3$ $18 \div 3$ $8 \div 2$ $9 \div 3$ $40 \div 5$ $36 \div 4$

$50 \div 10$ $15 \div 5$ $30 \div 5$ $20 \div 4$ $16 \div 2$ $21 \div 3$

Remember

Use facts that you already know, like tables facts or other division facts.

Equal parts

A **fraction** is part of something that has been split into equal pieces.

Halves

A **half** is one out of two equal pieces and is written $\frac{1}{2}$.
These have both been split into halves.

Quarters

A **quarter** is one out of four equal pieces and is written $\frac{1}{4}$.
These have both been split into quarters.

Three-quarters is three out of four equal pieces and is
written $\frac{3}{4}$.

Thirds

A **third** is one out of three equal pieces and is written $\frac{1}{3}$.
These have both been split into thirds.

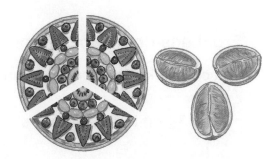

Test yourself

1. Which of these are split into halves?

a   b   c   d

Remember

Fractions are equal parts
of something. $\frac{1}{2}$, $\frac{1}{4}$, $\frac{3}{4}$ and
$\frac{1}{3}$ are all fractions.

Finding fractions

What fraction of these shapes is blue?

 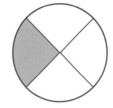 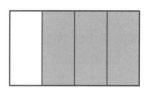

1 out of 2 equal parts is blue.	1 out of 4 equal parts is blue.	3 out of 4 equal parts are blue.

Answers $\frac{1}{2}$ is blue. $\frac{1}{4}$ is blue. $\frac{3}{4}$ is blue.

What fraction of the doughnut has been eaten?

Answers

$\frac{1}{2}$ of the doughnut has been eaten. $\frac{1}{4}$ of the doughnut has been eaten. $\frac{3}{4}$ of the doughnut has been eaten.

Remember

One of two equal parts is $\frac{1}{2}$.
One of four equal parts is $\frac{1}{4}$.

Fractions on a number line

You can mark a **fraction** on a number line.

Mark $3\frac{1}{2}$ on this number line

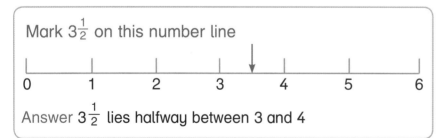

Answer $3\frac{1}{2}$ lies halfway between 3 and 4

Mark $7\frac{1}{2}$ on this number line

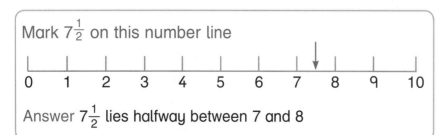

Answer $7\frac{1}{2}$ lies halfway between 7 and 8

Test yourself

1. What fraction of the windows is lit up?

a

b

Equivalent fractions

Equivalent fractions are fractions that have the same value, even though they are written differently.

One-half of this **square** is purple.

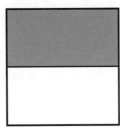

Two-quarters of this square are purple.

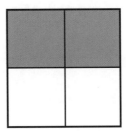

One-half of these sweets is ringed.

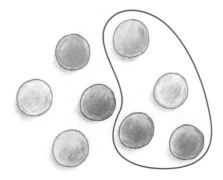

Two-quarters of these sweets are ringed.

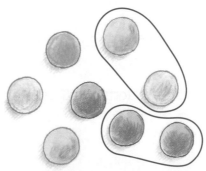

Can you see that one-half $\frac{1}{2}$ and two-quarters $\frac{2}{4}$ are the same?

Test yourself

1. Fold an A4 sheet of paper in half. Write $\frac{1}{2}$ on each piece.

2. Fold another A4 sheet of paper in half. Now fold it in half again. Write $\frac{1}{4}$ on each piece.

3. Colour one part of the first sheet of paper and two parts of the second. Have you coloured the same amount?

Remember

One-half $\frac{1}{2}$ and two-quarters $\frac{2}{4}$ are the same.

Fractions of numbers

Finding half of a number

Halving a number is dividing it by 2. If you know your ÷ 2 **division** facts (see page 28) then you can halve all the **even numbers** to 24.

18 ÷ 2 = 9 so half of 18 is 9

To halve larger numbers, split them up (partition them), like this.

$\frac{1}{2}$ of 34 =

Find half of 30 and half of 4, and add: 15 + 2 = 17

Answer 17

Finding one-quarter of a number

Finding a **quarter** of a number is dividing it by 4. If you know your ÷ 4 division facts (see page 28) then you can find one-quarter of all the **multiples** of 4 to 48.

32 ÷ 4 = 8 so one-quarter of 32 is 8

To find one-quarter of larger numbers, you can halve the number first and then halve the answer. This is because **half** of a half is one-quarter.

$\frac{1}{4}$ of 68 =

Find half of 68 first: half of 60 is 30 and half of 8 is 4, so half of 68 is 34.

Now halve 34 to find one-quarter: half of 34 is 17

Answer 17

Finding three-quarters of a number

First find one-quarter and then multiply the answer by 3.

$\frac{3}{4}$ of 40 =

Divide 40 by 4 to find one-quarter: 10

Then multiply the answer by 3 to give three-quarters: 10 × 3 = 30

Answer 30

Remember

To find half of a number, divide it by 2.

To find a quarter of a number, divide it by 4.

Test yourself

1. Answer these fraction questions.

   a $\frac{1}{2}$ of 20 $\frac{1}{4}$ of 20

      $\frac{3}{4}$ of 20

   b $\frac{1}{2}$ of 44 $\frac{1}{4}$ of 44

      $\frac{3}{4}$ of 44

   c $\frac{1}{2}$ of 72 $\frac{1}{4}$ of 72

      $\frac{3}{4}$ of 72

Number stories

A number story is a story in words that can also be written in numbers, as a number statement.

A cat has four legs. Five cats have 20 legs altogether.

This number story can be written as the number statement: 5 × 4 = 20

Emma has four cats, her sister has five cats. They have nine cats altogether.

Number statement: 4 + 5 = 9

Henry has eight cat treats. He shares them between his two cats. Each cat gets four treats.

Number statement: 8 ÷ 2 = 4

A packet of cat food cost 35p. George paid with a 50p coin.
He was given 15p change.

Number statement: 50 − 35 = 15

Make up number stories to match these statements.
You could think about stories with sweets, fruit, animals or money.

12 − 8 = 4   15 + 15 = 30   14 ÷ 2 = 7   5 × 3 = 15

Test yourself

1. Write the number statements.
   a Shani had 35p. She was given another 17p.
     She now has 52p.
   b A person has two legs. Seven people have 14 legs.
   c I had 16 sweets. I ate nine of them. I have seven left.
   d 20 children got into groups of two. There were
     10 groups.

Remember

Write number statements and practise making up your own number stories.

Number problems

To solve a number problem, first decide whether to add, subtract, multiply or divide.

A go-kart has four wheels. How many wheels do three go-karts have?

This can be written as   3 × 4 = ▢

Now work out the answer. You could add three lots of four or use times tables facts.

3 × 4 = 12

Answer 12 wheels

```
    4
    4
+   4
─────
  1 2
```

A go-kart ride cost 37p. Rose paid with a 50p coin. How much change was she given?

This can be written as 50 − 37 = ▢

Now work out the answer. You could count on from 37 up to 50, or subtract 37 from 50.

```
      +10p      + 3p
37p         47p        50p
```

50 − 37 = 13p

Answer 13p

(See page 37 for more on finding change.)

Test yourself

1. Ravi had 45p. He was given another 27p. How much has he now?

2. A bicycle has two wheels. How many wheels have eight bicycles?

3. I had 24 sweets. I ate nine. How many have I now?

4. 18 children got into groups of two. How many groups are there?

Remember

To solve a number problem, first decide whether to add, subtract, multiply or divide.

Questions with more than one answer

Some number problems and puzzles have more than one correct answer. As long as the answer you give is correct, it doesn't matter if someone else gives a different answer.

Look at the puzzle below.

Use some of these cards to make a correct number statement

You could give any of the following answers.

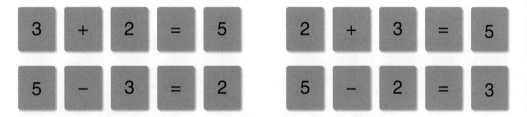

You could even put the equals sign here.

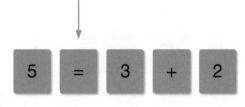

What is on one side of the equals sign is worth the same as what is on the other side, so it is correct.

Write two numbers with a sum of 12

'Sum' means 'total' or numbers added together.

Possible answers 11 and 1, 10 and 2, 9 and 3, 8 and 4, 7 and 5

Test yourself

1. Answer these questions.
   a Write two numbers with a sum of 15
   b Write two numbers with a difference of 3

2. Use some of these cards to make a correct number statement.

   a 4 5 8 1 = + +

   b 6 2 3 1 = × ÷

Remember

Don't worry if there is more than one answer. Make sure that the answer you give is correct.

Money

Make sure you know what each of these coins and notes is worth.

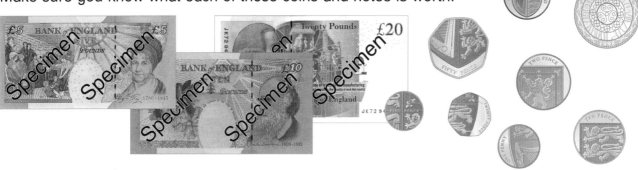

Paying exactly

You can pay for something exactly using different coins (without needing change).

You can buy these marshmallows using these coins…

…or these coins.

To find the smallest number of coins to pay for something costing 72p, follow the steps below.

1. Pick the largest coin that is worth less than the amount.

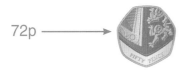
72p

2. See how much more is left to pay. 72p – 50p = 22p
Pick the largest coin that is worth less than this amount.

22p

3. See how much more is left to pay. 22p – 20p = 2p

2p

The smallest number of coins to pay 72p is 50p, 20p and 2p.

Test yourself

1. Find the totals of these coins.
   a 2p, 2p, 5p and 1p
   b £1, £2
   c 50p, 10p, 5p, 1p

2. Find the smallest number of coins to pay for these toys.

   a

   59p

   b

   34p

   c
   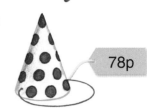
   78p

Working out change

Sometimes you don't have the exact money to pay for something. You might pay with a larger coin and be given change. Here are two ways to find out how much change you will be given.

1. Count on from the price until you get to the coin amount

32p $\xrightarrow{+ 8p}$ 40p $\xrightarrow{+ 10p}$

Answer **18p change**

2. Take away the price from the coin you gave

– 32p = 18p change

Answer **18p change**

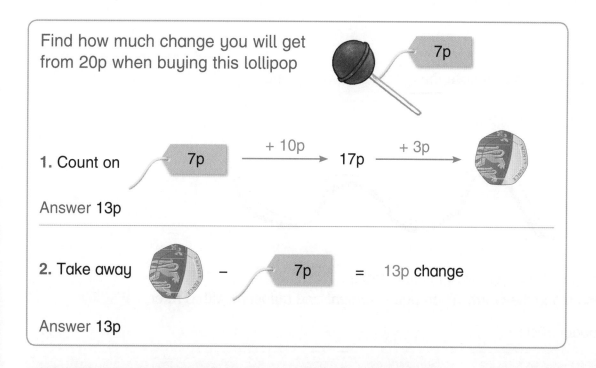

Find how much change you will get from 20p when buying this lollipop — 7p

1. Count on 7p $\xrightarrow{+ 10p}$ 17p $\xrightarrow{+ 3p}$

Answer **13p**

2. Take away – 7p = 13p change

Answer **13p**

Test yourself

1. How much change from 20p will you get when you buy something costing:
   a 6p   c 4p
   b 11p   d 17p

2. How much change from 50p will you get when you buy something costing:
   a 23p   d 42p
   b 14p   e 38p
   c 35p   f 19p

Remember

To find change:
- either count on from the price to the coin amount
- or take away the price from the coin amount.

Length

You find out how long something is by measuring its **length**. Length is measured in centimetres and metres.

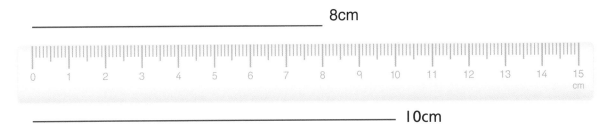

| centimetres |
| short things, like |
| pencils, hands, shoes |

| metres |
| long things, like the |
| floor, playground, hall |

There are 100 centimetres (cm) in a metre (m).

You can measure length with a ruler, tape measure, trundle wheel or metre stick. We use a ruler to measure these lines in centimetres, like this.

8cm

```
|||||||||||||||||||||||||||||||||||||||||||||||||||||||||||||||||||||||||||||||||||||||||||||||
  0    1    2    3    4    5    6    7    8    9    10   11   12   13   14   15
                                                                             cm
```

10cm

Always line up your ruler on the end of the line.

Estimating

You might be asked to **estimate** the length of a wiggly line.

How long do you think this wiggly worm is?

Try to imagine the wiggly worm pulled straight.
Lie a string along the worm. Then pull it straight and measure with a ruler.

Answer about 12cm

Test yourself

1. Measure the length of these lines.
   a _____ b

2. Estimate the length of this line.

Remember

Always line up your ruler on the end of the line.

There are 100 centimetres (cm) in a metre (m).

Mass

You find out how heavy something is by measuring its **mass**. Mass is sometimes called weight. Mass is measured in grams and kilograms.

> grams
> light things, like eggs, socks, books

> kilograms
> heavy things, like people, bags of sugar

There are 1000 grams (g) in a kilogram (kg).

Mass is measured with scales like these.

bathroom scales

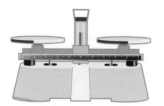

balance scales

kitchen scales

Remember

There are 1000 grams (g) in a kilogram (kg).

Test yourself

1. How heavy are these objects?

a

b

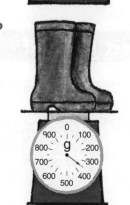

How heavy are these animals?

Answer The cat weighs $3\frac{1}{2}$kg and the guinea pig weighs 750g.

Estimating

Look at some objects around you, such as a book, a bag of potatoes – even yourself! Have a guess at their mass. Then weigh them to find out if your guesses were correct.

Capacity

You find out how much something holds by measuring its **capacity**. Capacity is measured in millilitres and litres.

millilitres
small containers, like cups, mugs, glasses

litres
large containers, like buckets, bowls, baths

There are 1000 millilitres (ml) in a litre (l).

Capacity can be measured using jugs and containers like these.

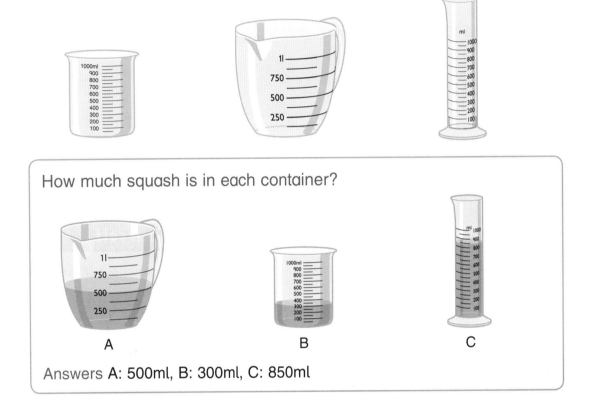

How much squash is in each container?

A   B   C

Answers A: 500ml, B: 300ml, C: 850ml

Estimating

Look at some containers around you, such as a cup, a bottle of lemonade and a sink. Have a guess at their capacity. Then find out whether your estimates were correct.

Test yourself

1. How much squash is in the jugs below?

a   b   c

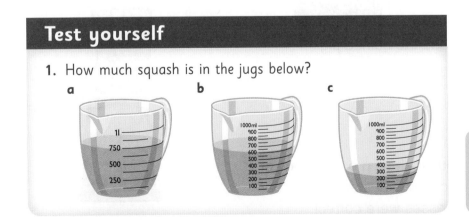

Remember

There are 1000 millilitres (ml) in a litre (l).

Adding and subtracting measures

When solving problems that include measurements, it can help to highlight or circle the numbers and the units of measurement (such as cm, kg, and so on).

Here they are highlighted in yellow.

Olivia uses 35cm of ribbon which she cuts from a length of ribbon that is 91cm long. How much ribbon is left?

Decide what you must do with the numbers and choose your method.

Subtract 35cm from 91cm, perhaps using a written method, like this.

	tens	ones
	$\cancel{9}^8$	^{11}
−	3	5
	5	6

Answer 56cm

Sasa puts 200g of butter, 500g of flour and 100g of sugar into a bowl. How much is in the bowl?

Answer 200g + 500g + 100g = 800g

Remember

Highlight or circle the numbers and units of measurement in the problem to make it easier.

Test yourself

1. **a** Ben cuts 37cm from a length of wood that is 74cm long. What length is left?
   b Ella is 45cm taller than Jack. Jack is 73cm tall. How tall is Ella?
   c David's cat weighs 8kg less than his dog. His dog weighs 13kg. How heavy is his cat?

Comparing measures

When you compare **lengths**, **masses** or **capacities**, always look at the units first to make sure they are the same.

Which is larger, 53m or 48m?

Here both measures are in metres. If the units are the same, then compare the numbers. 53 is larger than 48, so 53m is larger than 48m.

Answer **53m is larger than 48m**

Using the < or > signs

To show which measure is larger or smaller, use the < (less than) or > (greater than) signs. When using the < or > signs, remember that the wider part of the sign is next to the larger number (see page 11).

53m > 48m   92g < 98g

Show which measure is larger using the < or > signs

73ml ___ 69ml

Answer **73ml > 69ml**

Show which measure is smaller using the < or > signs

81kg ___ 66kg

Answer **81kg > 66kg**

Test yourself

1. Show which measure in each pair is larger using the < or > signs.
   a 66kg ___ 81kg   **c** 95m ___ 97m
   b 68cm ___ 33cm   **d** 44ml ___ 50ml

2. Show which measure in each pair is larger using the < or > signs. Make sure you check the units.
   a 1kg ___ 1g   **c** 50l ___ 50ml
   b 2cm ___ 2m   **d** 5kg ___ 50g

Remember

If the units are not the same, think carefully about which is larger.

Comparing lengths of time

You will need to use this information when comparing lengths of time.

60 seconds = 1 minute

60 minutes = 1 hour

24 hours = 1 day

7 days = 1 week

52 weeks = 1 year

MARCH

				1	2	3
4	5	6	7	8	9	10
11	12	13	14	15	16	17
18	19	20	21	22	23	24
25	26	27	28	29	30	31

Which is the longer length of time: 1 week or 5 days?

First, look carefully at the units. Here they are weeks and days. Find the relationship between these units (7 days = 1 week) to help you decide which is longer. Here 1 week is longer because 7 days is longer than 5 days.

Answer **1 week**

Which is the shorter length of time: 50 seconds or 1 minute?

Find the relationship between these seconds and minutes (60 seconds = 1 minute) to help you decide which is shorter. Here 50 seconds is shorter because 50 seconds is shorter than 60 seconds.

Answer **50 seconds**

Which is the longer length of time: 25 hours or 1 day?

24 hours = 1 day. So 25 hours is longer because it is longer than 1 day (which is only 24 hours).

Answer **25 hours**

Days

Learn the names of the days in order.

Monday
Tuesday
Wednesday
Thursday
Friday
Saturday
Sunday

Months

Learn the names of the months in order.

January
February
March
April
May
June
July
August
September
October
November
December

Remember

Learn the relationship between different measurements of time so you can compare them.

Test yourself

1. Which is longer?
   - **a** 20 hours or 1 day
   - **b** 50 minutes or 1 hour
   - **c** 55 weeks or 1 year
   - **d** 1 minute or 100 seconds

2. Which is shorter?
   - **a** 1 hour or 45 minutes
   - **b** 1 week or 10 days
   - **c** 1 year or 50 weeks
   - **d** 1 minute or 70 seconds

Telling the time

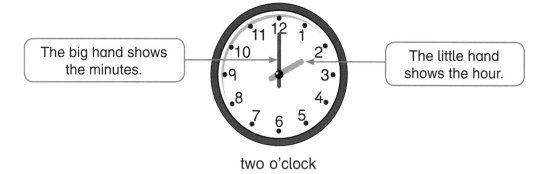

The big hand shows the minutes.

The little hand shows the hour.

two o'clock

quarter past two

This is 'quarter past' because the big hand has gone round one-quarter of the clock.

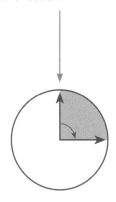

half past two

This is 'half past' because the big hand has gone round one-half of the clock.

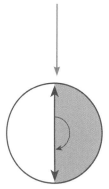

quarter to three

This is 'quarter to' because the big hand has gone round three-quarters of the clock and it has one-quarter to go.

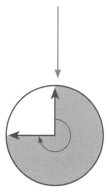

Test yourself

1. What time does each clock show?

a

b

c

The number the little hand is nearest to shows the hour.

The hour hand is just past two. The time is quarter past two.

The hour hand is nearly at five. The time is quarter to five.

The big hand shows how many minutes to or past the hour.

It's ten minutes past five.

It's twenty minutes to seven.

> between two numbers there are five minutes

Can you tell the time on these clocks?

Answers

It's twenty-five minutes past seven.

It's five minutes to nine.

It's twenty-five to four.

> sometimes the word 'minutes' is missed out

Test yourself

1. What time do these clocks show?

a

b

c

Remember

The number the little hand is nearest to shows the hour.

The big hand shows how many minutes to or past the hour.

2-D shapes

2-D shapes are flat shapes without thickness.

You need to know the names of these 2-D shapes and some facts about each one.

Circle

A **circle** has one curved side.

Triangle

Triangles have three straight sides.

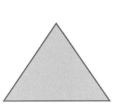 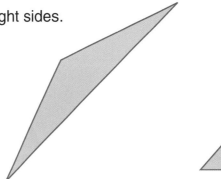 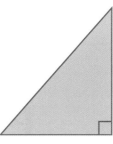

Rectangle

All **rectangles** have four **right angles** and four straight sides

Square

A **square** has four right angles and four sides of equal **length**.

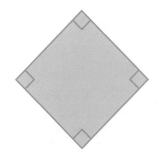 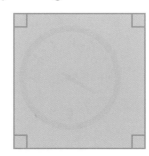

Pentagon

Pentagons have five straight sides.

 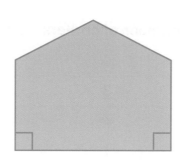 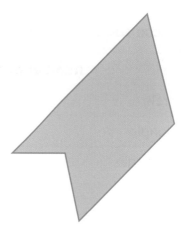

Hexagon

All **hexagons** have six straight sides.

 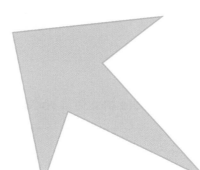 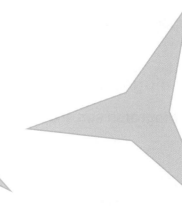

Octagon

An **octagon** has eight straight sides.

 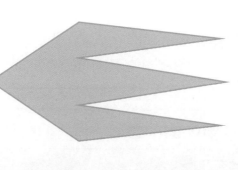 

Test yourself

1. Get a piece of paper, a ruler and a pencil. Cover the shapes on this page. Draw:
   a a triangle   **b** a square   **c** an octagon.

2. Which shape am I? I have:
   a four right angles and four straight sides of equal length
   b one curved side
   c six straight sides
   d five straight sides.

Remember

2-D shapes are flat shapes. They can have curved or straight sides.

Sorting 2-D shapes

You can sort shapes by their sides and corners (**vertices**).

	number of sides	number of corners	straight or curved?
circle	1	0	curved
triangle	3	3	straight
rectangle	4	4	straight
square	4	4	straight
pentagon	5	5	straight
hexagon	6	6	straight
octagon	8	8	straight

Venn diagrams

Venn diagrams sort shapes using a **circle** inside a **rectangle**, like this.

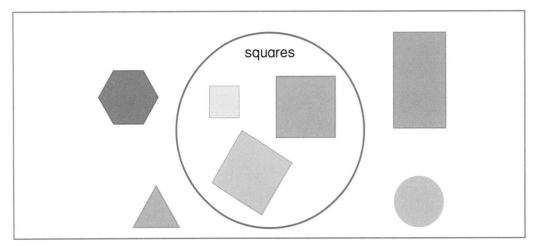

Which of these shapes is in the wrong place?

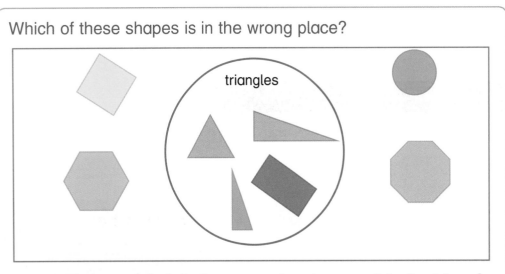

Answer The rectangle is in the wrong place because it isn't a **triangle**.

Carroll diagrams

Carroll diagrams sort shapes inside rectangles. The headings are always something and its opposite (like 'squares and not squares' or 'circles and not circles').

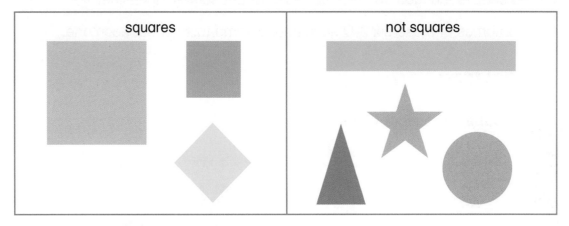

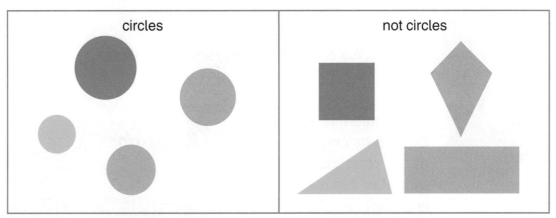

Test yourself

1. Which of these shapes is in the wrong place?

   a 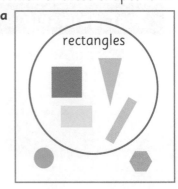   b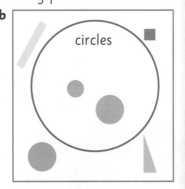

2. Which of these shapes is in the wrong place?

   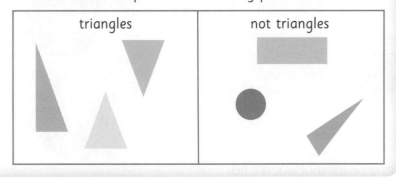

Remember

Venn diagrams are used to sort data. They are made up of one or more circles inside a rectangle.

Carroll diagrams are made from rectangles. They always show one type of thing and its opposite.

3-D shapes

3-D shapes are solid shapes that you can pick up, hold, or put something inside.

You need to know the names of these six 3-D shapes and some facts about each one.

3-D shapes with flat faces

A **cube** has square **faces**.

A **cuboid** has rectangular faces.

A **pyramid** has one face that can be any shape. All the other faces are **triangles** that meet together at a point.

> ### Remember
> Shapes with flat faces include: cubes, cuboids and pyramids.
>
> Shapes with curved faces include: spheres, cones and cylinders.

3-D shapes with curved faces

A **sphere** is like a ball.

A **cone** has a circular face and a point.

A **cylinder** is like a tube with a circular face at each end.

Test yourself

1. Name these shapes.

   a

   b

   c

Describing 3-D shapes

You can describe 3-D shapes by looking at the number of **faces**, **edges** and **vertices** that each one has.

Faces are the surfaces making up the shape. They are **2-D shapes** and can be flat or curved.

Edges are the lines where the faces meet. If you make a 3-D skeleton using straws, the straws are the edges of the shape.

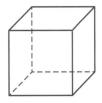

Vertices are where the edges join together at a point.

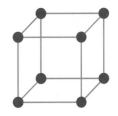

Cubes and cuboids

Cubes and cuboids have 6 flat faces (rectangular or square), 12 edges and 8 vertices.

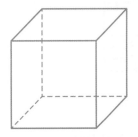
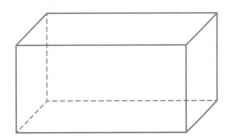

Sphere

A sphere has 1 curved face, no edges and no vertices.

Cone

A cone has 1 circular flat face and 1 curved face. It has 1 edge and 1 vertex.

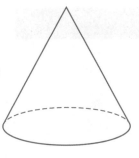

Remember

Find some 3-D shapes around your home (such as a cereal packet or a football). Practise counting and describing the faces, edges and vertices.

Test yourself

1. Describe the faces, edges and vertices of these shapes.

a

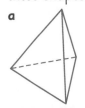

b

c

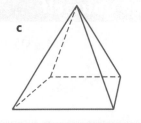

Symmetry

A shape or pattern is symmetrical when it has one or more lines of **symmetry**. Look at the examples below.

Kite

This has one line of symmetry.
The two halves match. It is symmetrical.

line of symmetry

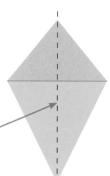

Flag

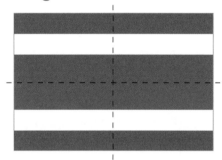

This flag has two lines of symmetry. If this shape was folded along one of the lines, the two halves would match. It is symmetrical.

Cross

This cross has four lines of symmetry. If this shape was folded along each of the lines, the two halves would always match. It is symmetrical.

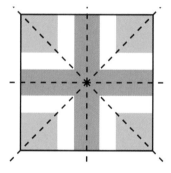

Cloud

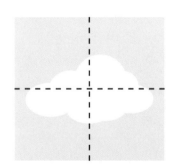

This picture of a cloud is different from the shapes above.

Imagine it folded in half. Whichever way you fold it, the two halves do not match, so it is not symmetrical.

Copying patterns

Copy this pattern. Colour the other side of the mirror line to make it symmetrical.

mirror line

It will help you if you imagine that the coloured squares are wet paint. Imagine that the paper is being folded along the mirror line. The wet paint will stick to the paper. Where would it go?

Think like this:

mirror line

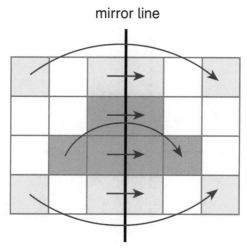

You can check your pattern with a mirror. Place the mirror along the line. Is the reflection you have drawn the same as the one in the mirror?

Test yourself

1. Copy these circle patterns. Make them symmetrical.

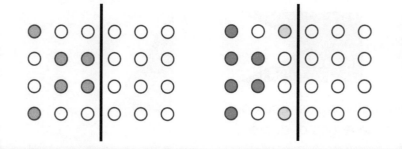

Remember

Check your pattern with a mirror.

Right angles and turns

An **angle** is a part of a turn. A **right angle** can also be called a quarter turn.

Look at these arrows.

A quarter turn goes through one right angle.

A half turn or a straight line goes through two right angles.

A complete turn goes through four right angles.

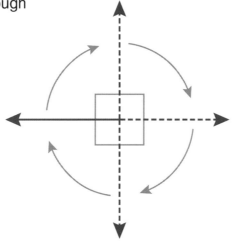

Remember

A right angle is nothing to do with 'right' or 'left'. It can be in any direction.

Learn the right angles in shapes like these.

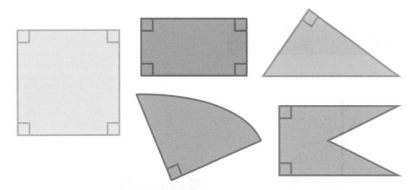

The outside corners of this page are right angles. Look out for more of them around you, like at the edges of doors and windows.

Test yourself

1. Tick the right angles. Not every shape has a right angle.

Positions

You can describe positions using words like these.

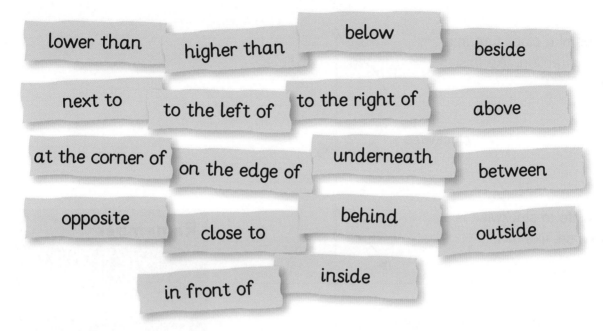

lower than · higher than · below · beside · next to · to the left of · to the right of · above · at the corner of · on the edge of · underneath · between · opposite · close to · behind · outside · in front of · inside

How to remember left and right

If you find it difficult to remember left and right, think of the capital letter L.

Push away with your hands – the left hand shows the capital letter L.

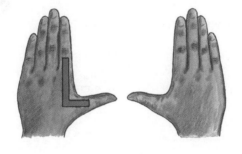

Describe where the robot is in this picture, using some of the words above

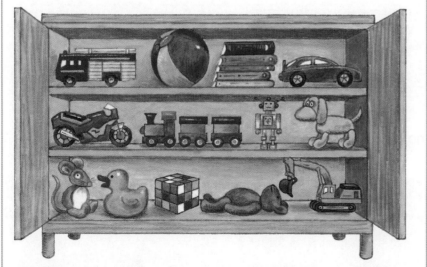

Answer **underneath the books, to the right of the train, to the left of the dog, above the bear, inside the cupboard**

Test yourself

1. What item is:
   a to the right of the cup
   b under the glove
   c to the left of the light bulb
   d below the shoe
   e between the cake and the pen
   f above the spoon?

Rotating

Rotating means turning. Rotating can be in a **clockwise** or **anticlockwise** direction.

The hands of a clock turn in a clockwise direction, like this.

clockwise

The opposite to clockwise is anticlockwise, like this.

anticlockwise

Remember

Turning to the right is a clockwise turn.

Turning to the left is anticlockwise.

The card pattern is rotating clockwise through quarter turns.

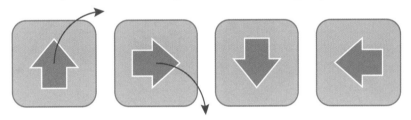

The card pattern is rotating anticlockwise through quarter turns.

How is the card pattern rotating here?

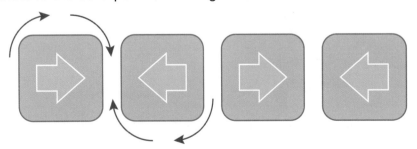

It is rotating clockwise through half turns.

Test yourself

1. Is this clockwise or anticlockwise?

   a

   b

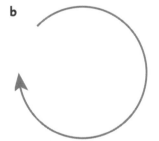

2. Is this card pattern rotating through quarter turns clockwise or anticlockwise?

Tally charts

You can can collect **data** and put it in a table.

To record data we can use **tallying**, like this |||. Every line stands for one thing.

A tally chart of the favourite crisps of Class 2

flavour	tally	total
ready salted	||||	4
cheese and onion	|||	3
salt and vinegar	||||||	6
prawn cocktail	|||||	5

In this tally chart one line stands for one child.

You can make the tallies easier to count by grouping them in fives, like this: ‖‖†

The fifth tally goes across four lines to show a 'bundle of five'.

These marks show eight things.   ‖‖† ||| 5 + 3 = 8

A tally chart of the pets of children in Class 2

pet	tally	total
snake	|||	3
cat	‖‖† |||	8
dog	‖‖† ‖‖† |	11
rabbit	||||	4

Test yourself

1. Some children have been asked to say what their favourite zoo animal is.

   Draw a tally chart of their answers.

lion	elephant	lion	giraffe	tiger
tiger	tiger	zebra	tiger	elephant
lion	zebra	zebra	tiger	giraffe	lion

Pictograms

A **pictogram** uses pictures of things, as in the examples below (data from page 57).

Pictogram of the favourite crisps of Class 2

Ready salted

Cheese and onion

Salt and vinegar

Prawn cocktail

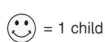 = 1 child

Pictogram of the pets of children in Class 2

Snake

Cat

Dog

Rabbit

⬜ = 1 child

How many children in Class 2 have a cat?

Count the squares to find out the answer.

Answer 8

Test yourself

1. Look at the pictogram of the favourite crisps of Class 2.
   How many children chose:
   a ready salted
   b salt and vinegar?

2. Look at the pictogram of the pets of children in Class 2.
   How many children have:
   a a snake
   b a dog?

Remember

Pictograms use pictures of things to show information.

Block diagrams

In a **block diagram**, blocks are joined up to make towers, as in the examples below (data from page 57).

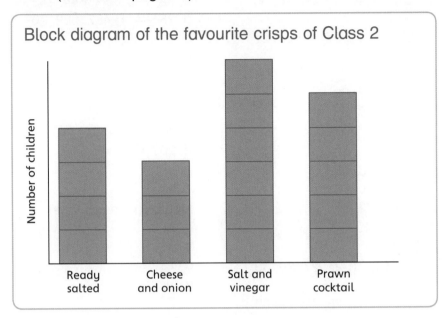

Block diagram of the favourite crisps of Class 2

Number of children

Ready salted   Cheese and onion   Salt and vinegar   Prawn cocktail

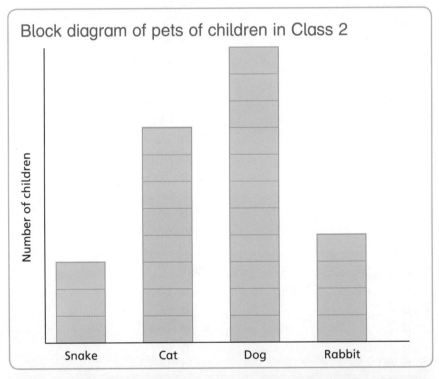

Block diagram of pets of children in Class 2

Number of children

Snake   Cat   Dog   Rabbit

Test yourself

1. In Class 2, which was the:
   a most popular flavour of crisps
   b least popular flavour of crisps?

2. In Class 2, how many children have:
   a a cat
   b a rabbit?

Remember

Block diagrams use blocks joined up to make towers that show information.

Answers

Page 4

1 a twelve
  b twenty-four
  c thirty-six
  d eighty-four
  e eighteen
  f forty-eight
  g one hundred
2 a 13
  b 200
  c 52
  d 95
  e 3000
  f 60

Page 5

1 a even
  b odd
  c odd
  d even
  e even
  f odd
  g even
  h odd
2 123, 659, 597, 365, 471

Page 6

1 a 40, 41, 42
  b 69, 68, 67
  c 89, 90, 91
  d 96, 95, 94

Page 7

1 46, 48, 50, 52, 54, 56, 58, 60, 62, 64, 66, 68, 70, 72, 74, 76
2 53, 51, 49, 47, 45, 43, 41, 39, 37
3 a 44, 46, 48
  b 67, 65, 63
  c 89, 91, 93
  d 92, 90, 88

Page 8

1 26, 36, 46, 56, 66, 76, 86, 96
2 87, 77, 67, 57, 47, 37, 27, 17, 7

3 a 78, 88, 98
  b 59, 49, 39

Page 9

1 a 58, 63, 68
  b 75, 70, 65
  c 67, 72, 77

Page 10

1 15, 18, 21, 24, 27, 30, 33, 36, 39
2 87, 84, 81, 78, 75, 72, 69, 66, 63, 60
3 48

Page 11

1 a <
  b >
  c <
  d >
2 a >
  b =
  c <
  d >

Page 12

1 a 13, 39, 52, 64, 73
  b 21, 42, 47, 69, 79
2 a 5
  b 3
3 a *40 + 6*
  b 80 + 4
  c 90 + 3
4 a 45 < 54
  b 81 > 76

Page 13

1 a 72, 193, 379, 644, 743
  b 251, 411, 487, 629, 709
2 a 5
  b 7
  c 2
3 a *100 + 40 + 6*
  b 400 + 30 + 9
  c 700 + 20 + 1
  d 200 + 90 + 7

Page 14

1 (approximate answers)
  a 3
  b 30
  c 15
  d 30

Page 15

1 a 9
  b 32, 42
  c 63, 59
  d 18, 33

Page 16

1 a 20 + 9
  b 40 + 6
  c 70 + 8
2 a 39
  b 41
  c 63

Page 17

1 a 53
  b 68
2 a 245
  b 487
3 a 15
  b 22

Page 18

1 a 95
  b 89
  c 85
2 8

Page 19

1 a 109
   b 151
   c 517
   d 471
2 7 and 7

Page 20

1 a +
   b −
   c −
   d +
2 a 41
   b 41
   c 46

Page 21

1 a 57
   b 66
   c 79
2 a 275
   b 503
   c 899
3 a 5
   b 7
   c 7

Page 22

1 a 11
   b 33
   c 36
2 6

Page 23

1 a 322
   b 718
   c 479
   d 41
2 5 and 5

Page 24

1 a 6
   b 1
   c 2
   d 7
2 a 9
   b 16
   c 7
   d 8
3 a 20
   b 60
   c 70

Page 25

1 a *4 x 2*
   b 4 x 5
   c 5 x 3
   d 3 x 4

Page 26

1 Check the answers against the times tables facts on page 26.

Page 27

1 a 2
   b 2
   c 3
   d 3
2 a 5
   b 3
   c 4
   d 4

Page 28

1 Check the answers against the division facts on page 28.

Page 29

1 a and d

Page 30

1 a $\frac{5}{10}$, which is the same as $\frac{1}{2}$
   b $\frac{9}{12}$, which is the same as $\frac{3}{4}$

Page 31

3 Yes, $\frac{1}{2}$ of the first piece is coloured in, and $\frac{1}{4} + \frac{1}{4}$ of the second piece is also coloured in ($\frac{1}{4} + \frac{1}{4} = \frac{1}{2}$).

Page 32

1 a 10   5   15
   b 22   11   33
   c 36   18   54

Page 33

1 a 35 + 17 = 52
   b 7 x 2 = 14
   c 16 − 9 = 7
   d 20 ÷ 2 = 10

Page 34

1 72p
2 16
3 15
4 9

Page 35

1 a for example 7 and 8
   b for example 9 and 6
2 a for example 4 + 5 = 8 + 1 or 4 + 1 = 5
   b for example 2 x 3 = 6 or 6 ÷ 2 = 3

Page 36

1 a 10p
   b £3
   c 66p
2 a 50p + 5p + 2p + 2p
   b 20p + 10p + 2p + 2p
   c 50p + 20p + 5p + 2p + 1p

Page 37

1 a 14p
   b 9p
   c 16p
   d 3p
2 a 27p
   b 36p
   c 15p
   d 8p
   e 12p
   f 31p

Page 38

1 a 3cm
   b 4cm
2 8cm

Page 39

1 a $4\frac{1}{2}$kg
   b 350g

Page 40

1 a 750ml
   b 600ml
   c 250ml

Page 41

1 **a** 37cm
   b 118cm
   c 5kg

Page 42

1 **a** <
   b >
   c <
   d <
2 **a** >
   b <
   c >
   d >

Page 43

1 **a** 1 day
   b 1 hour
   c 55 weeks
   d 100 seconds
2 **a** 1 hour
   b 10 days
   c 1 year
   d 70 seconds

Page 44

1 **a** 4:15 (quarter past four)
   b 4:30 (half past four)
   c 4:45 (quarter to five)

Page 45

1 **a** 9:15 (quarter past nine)
   b 3:40 (twenty to four)
   c 10:20 (twenty past ten)

Page 47

1 Check the shapes against the pictures on pages 46–47.
2 **a** square
   b circle
   c hexagon
   d pentagon

Page 49

1 **a** There is a green triangle inside the ring.
   b There is a blue circle that should be inside the ring.
2 There is a blue triangle in the 'not triangles' section.

Page 50

1 **a** cube
   b sphere (ball)
   c pyramid

Page 51

1 **a** 4 faces, 6 edges, 4 vertices
   b 3 faces, 2 edges, 0 vertices
   c 5 faces, 8 edges, 5 vertices,

Page 52

1 **b** and **c**

Page 53

1 This is how the patterns should look. It doesn't matter if the colours aren't exactly the same.

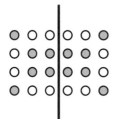

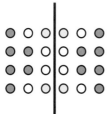

Page 54

Page 55

1 **a** pen
   b light bulb
   c scooter
   d ball
   e cup
   f cake

Page 56

1 **a** anticlockwise
   b clockwise
2 clockwise

Page 57

animal	tally	total
lion	IIII	4
tiger	IIII	5
elephant	II	2
zebra	III	3
giraffe	II	2

Page 58

1 **a** 4
   b 6
2 **a** 3
   b 11

Page 59

1 **a** Salt and vinegar
   b Cheese and onion
2 **a** 8
   b 4

Glossary

2-D shapes	flat shapes without thickness
3-D shapes	solid or hollow shapes that you can pick up or hold
addition	joining together numbers or things to make totals. These are all words that can mean **addition**: more, add, plus, sum, total, altogether, and. This sign means **addition** +.
angle	part of a turn
anticlockwise	the opposite direction to **clockwise**
block diagram	a type of graph that uses blocks joined together to show **data**
capacity	how much something holds – **capacity** is measured in millilitres (ml) and litres (l)
Carroll diagram	a diagram used to sort **data** – it always has something and its opposite, like 'red' and 'not red' or 'even' and 'not even'
circle	a **2-D shape** with one curved side
clockwise	the hands of a clock turn in a **clockwise** direction
cone	a **3-D shape** with a circular **face** and a point
cube	a **3-D shape** with **square faces**
cuboid	a **3-D shape** with rectangular **faces**
cylinder	a **3-D shape** like a tube with a circular **face** at each end
data	information
digits	the 10 symbols we use to write numbers (0, 1, 2, 3, 4, 5, 6, 7, 8 and 9)
division	sharing or sorting things into equal groups
edges	the lines where the **faces** of a **3-D shape** meet – if you make the skeleton of a **3-D shape** using straws, the straws are the **edges** of the shape
equivalent fractions	**fractions** with the same value that are written differently ($\frac{1}{2}$ and $\frac{2}{4}$)
estimate	to make a 'good guess'
even number	any number that is divided by 2 without a **remainder** – all **even numbers** end in 0, 2, 4, 6 or 8
faces	the surfaces that make up a **3-D shape** – **faces** are **2-D shapes** and can be flat or curved
fraction	part of something that has been split into equal parts
half	one part of something split into two equal parts
hexagon	a **2-D shape** with six straight sides
length	how long something is – **length** is measured in centimetres (cm) and metres (m)

mass	how heavy an object is – **mass** is measured in grams (g) and kilograms (kg)
multiple	a number that is in a times table – **multiples** of 3 are 3, 6, 9, 12, 15, 18, 21, 24, 27, 30, 33, 36, 39 and they carry on and on in threes
multiplication	a quick way of adding the same number many times – the sign × means **multiplication**
octagon	a **2-D shape** with eight straight sides
odd number	any number that, when divided by 2, has a **remainder** of 1 – all **odd numbers** end in 1, 3, 5, 7 or 9
pentagon	a **2-D shape** with five straight sides
pictogram	diagrams used to show **data** – they use pictures of things
pyramid	a **3-D shape** with one **face** that can be any shape and all the other **faces** are **triangles** that meet together at a point
quarter	one part of something split into four equal parts
rectangle	a **2-D shape** with four **right angles** and four straight sides
remainder	what is left over when one number is divided by another number
right angle	a quarter turn – there are four **right angles** in a full turn
sequence	numbers arranged in a special order
sphere	a **3-D shape** that is like a ball
square	a **2-D shape** with four **right angles** and four sides of equal **length**
subtraction	taking away part of a group of things or a number. These are all words that can mean **subtraction**: subtract, take away, less than, minus, difference between, fewer. This sign – means **subtraction**.
symmetry	a shape has **symmetry** (is symmetrical) when it is the same on both sides of a line
tallying	a way of recording **data** with lines like this: III Each line stands for one of the things being counted. Sometimes **tallying** is used to make a tally chart.
third	one part of something split into three equal parts
triangle	a **2-D shape** with three straight sides
Venn diagram	a diagram used to sort **data** – it shows things that belong in one or more sets
vertices	a corner of a **3-D shape** where **edges** meet – one corner is known as a vertex